Original title:
Roots Beneath the Surface

Copyright © 2025 Creative Arts Management OÜ
All rights reserved.

Author: Alec Davenport
ISBN HARDBACK: 978-1-80581-790-1
ISBN PAPERBACK: 978-1-80581-317-0
ISBN EBOOK: 978-1-80581-790-1

Resonance of the Unseen

In the ground they wiggle and twist,
A secret world that often gets missed.
They dance with glee, just out of sight,
Throwing a party, deep in the night.

The worms wear hats, and the fungi sing,
Earth's hidden jesters, doing their thing.
They share wild tales of the plants above,
In a rhythm of laughter, all wrapped in love.

While daisies bloom, they are quite aware,
Of the underground circus, a comical fair.
With roots for swings, and soil for the stage,
They perform their acts, in a joyful rage.

So if you glance down, don't be surprised,
By the quirky fun where life's disguised.
For laughter echoes in the dirt below,
With a secret world, putting on a show!

The Pulse Beneath

In the garden where the gnomes dance,
Whispers from the soil take their stance.
Worms gossip secrets of the juicy fruit,
While ants hold parades in their tiny hoot.

Puddles laugh as they soak up the sun,
And daisies plot to steal the fun.
Even the beetles wear tiny clothes,
As they boogie in rows, striking a pose.

Heartstrings in the Dark

The moonlight tickles the roots below,
While dreams of radishes put on a show.
Frogs croak out lullabies sweet and low,
Their chorus a jest in the night's soft glow.

Sneaky squirrels throw acorn balls,
And crickets chirp their late-night calls.
Even shadows have a giggle or two,
As they prance 'round the great old yew.

The Weaving of Lives

Woven tales in the tangled grass,
Where spy bugs gather to hold their class.
Laughter bubbles from the hidden glade,
As grasshoppers sing with a sweet serenade.

Each blade sways with a purpose so bold,
Sharing stories that never get old.
Mice write novels in the evening mist,
Filling pages no one can resist.

Patterns in the Loam

In the squishy earth, surprises sprout,
Jokester mushrooms play peekaboo out.
Fungi giggle at the tales they weave,
While sunflowers plot how to deceive.

Wiggly paths chart a dance unknown,
As earthworms play checkers on a throne.
The soil hums tunes of laughter and cheer,
In a world where every critter's sincere.

The Mystery of the Hidden Grove

In the quiet shade where no one peeks,
Live the spunky gnomes who play hide and seek.
With mushroom hats and dancing feet,
They giggle and wiggle, oh, what a treat!

But just as they think they've outsmarted the sun,
A squirrel drops acorns, and their fun's undone.
They scramble in chaos, their laughter contagious,
While the wise old tree shakes its branches outrageous!

Lingering Lives in the Loam

Deep in the dirt where the worms do squirm,
You'd find a party beyond the norm.
With earthworms dancing and moles in a race,
They chuckle and joke in their underground space.

A tortoise in a tutu comes wiggling through,
While crickets provide a top-notch review.
Each time they all tumble, they find it a blast,
Proving that fun doesn't need to be fast!

The Concealed Garden's Secrets

In a garden so lush, with veggies galore,
Tomatoes gossip, and carrots implore.
The radishes roll their eyes at the peas,
Who think they're the stars of this leafy tease.

At night, the moon laughs with shadows that dance,
While butterflies twirl in a swirling trance.
Each bloom tells a tale of its day in the sun,
As the zucchini jokes about being 'well-done!'

Threads Woven in Silence

Beneath the still soil, where secrets reside,
A chatty old spider spins webs with pride.
Her stories are wild, from the past to the now,
While ants sip on tea, trying to know how.

The beetles all nod, quite thrilled at the scheme,
As butterflies flutter, lost in a dream.
In this hidden realm, laughter echoes so clear,
Where every critter has a joke and a cheer!

The Dark Ballet of Mycelium

In shadows thick, the fungus twirls,
A dance of spores, a secret swirl.
With pirouettes in damp, dark soil,
They play like jesters, never toil.

Mushrooms chuckle, hats too tall,
They flip and flop, not worried at all.
With every jig, they whisper low,
The hidden giggles that only they know.

Where Forgotten Dreams Flourish

In corners where the wild things grow,
Lies a treasure of dreams, just below.
Old wishes snooze beneath the ground,
While sleepy worms hum a quirky sound.

They doze and stretch in the earthy bed,
Chatting softly in dreams long dead.
With every wiggle, they weave and plea,
To remind us of what used to be.

Beneath the Crust of Time

Under layers thick, in silence deep,
The ancient giggles start to creep.
Time travelers lost, in dirt they bask,
With mischief ready, no need to ask.

They hiccup laughs from days of yore,
Past the stones and roots they explore.
In this muddy maze of cheeky schemes,
Lies the echo of our silliest dreams.

The Underground Symphony

The bugs convene for a grand old show,
With beetles dancing and crickets in tow.
In earthy halls, the music plays,
A vibrant beat that sways and sways.

From twinkling ants to the grumpy worms,
They tap their feet, ignoring the terms.
The underground thrives with laughter and cheer,
A concert of quirks, for all to hear.

Whispered Histories

In the garden, gossip grows,
Tomatoes chat with carrots, you know.
Each onion has a tale to tell,
While radishes laugh, 'Oh, isn't that swell?'

The daisies dance, the daisies prance,
Spilling secrets in a colorful trance.
'Did you hear what the rhubarb said?'
'Yeah, it's all the buzz, right from its bed!'

The Ground's Embrace

Beneath the sod, there's quite a scene,
Worms throw parties, a squiggly routine.
The moles DJ, beat drops like a stone,
While beetles groove, in their tiny zone.

Cabbages gossip, zucchini joins in,
'Did you see what the radish wore, with a grin?'
The soil's a club where the vegetables sing,
Underground nightlife, oh what joy they bring!

Conduits of Existence

Down below, the fibers weave,
They giggle and chuckle, never leave.
'Hey, do you know that old oak tree?'
'Yeah, it's got a history, wild as can be!'

The dandelions plot, 'Let's float away!'
While the grass rolls its eyes, 'Not today!'
Through tangled paths, they share their lore,
In the tangled mess, there's never a bore!

Shadows of the Ancients

Beneath the lilacs, scribes of old,
Penning down stories in whispers bold.
'Did you hear what that fungus said?'
'No, but I bet it's full of dread!'

Ancient roots chuckle, nodding in time,
While sprouting green tells tales in rhyme.
The shadows giggle, hiding from light,
'Let's not resurface; it's safer at night!'

The Unseen Connection

In the garden, gnomes conspire,
Whisper secrets, never tire.
They chat about the plants' wild dreams,
While plotting pranks and silly schemes.

Beneath the ground, they take delight,
In mischief made both day and night.
With carrots dressed in silly hats,
And dancing beans that play with cats.

Socks left out that seem to dance,
Unseen forces in this chance.
The hedgehogs laugh, the bunnies cheer,
While worms just wiggle in good cheer.

But when the sun begins to set,
The gnomes retreat—yet don't you fret!
For in the dark, they base their plans,
To tickle toes of sleeping fans.

Intertwined Shadows

In twilight's glow, the shadows meet,
Twist and twirl on tiny feet.
A dance of laughter, slight and spry,
They tickle grass and brush the sky.

The squirrels plan a nutty heist,
In whispers shared, oh so enticed.
While owls play chess and throw in jokes,
As moonlight bathes the little folks.

Underneath the towering trees,
The critters giggle in the breeze.
An unseen game of hide and seek,
Amid the laughter, they all squeak.

And when the stars begin to shine,
They toast with acorns, sip on wine.
For night's the time for silliness,
In shadows' grasp, there's no distress.

Beneath the Canopy

Under leaves, the critters chat,
A party planned for them to bat.
With twinkling lights and snacks galore,
They'll have a blast, they'll laugh and roar.

The raccoons set up disco balls,
While songbirds harmonize with calls.
The moles provide the dance floor space,
As fireflies join, keeping their pace.

The bunnies break out in a jig,
While prancing around a giant fig.
With every leap, a giggling sound,
In this grand bash beneath the ground.

And when the sun begins to peek,
They all disperse, it's not for sneak.
They leave a note with laughter penned,
"Until next time, dear furry friends!"

Murmurs in the Dark

In shadows deep, the whispers start,
Made by creatures with a heart.
A hedgehog hums a silly tune,
As crickets join beneath the moon.

The mice exchange their daring tales,
Of cheese delights and winding trails.
While cats pretend to snooze so sound,
Yet can't resist the giggles found.

An owl perched high, a wise old sage,
Chuckles softly, turns the page.
On stories of enchanted nights,
When stars ignited playful sights.

Through murky paths, they frolic free,
Sharing laughs beneath the tree.
In darkness, joy and fun collide,
As friendship blooms, their hearts reside.

Dark Roots of Connection

In the garden where secrets dwell,
Mischievous whispers, they cast a spell.
Worms debate over who's the best,
While mischief thrives in their humble nest.

Gossip flows through soil like tea,
Raccoons throw parties, oh what glee!
Each creature jives in a rhythmic trance,
Branching out, giving nature a chance.

Squirrels plot with acorns in hand,
As roots stretch out, making their land.
They chuckle and chatter, what a sight,
In shadows that dance under moonlight.

So if you dig, be sure to smile,
For the underground crew is worth your while.
With humor as fresh as morning dew,
Connections bloom, just like new shoes.

The Cradle of Life

In a patch of dirt, dreams take their flight,
Tiny seeds plot under the moonlight.
Wiggly worms host a dance so spry,
While ants gossip, they never are shy.

A plump potato dreams of its fate,
Unbeknownst to it, it's tempting the plate.
"Pass the butter!" the veggies all cheer,
While roots giggle, "We're safe down here!"

Ladybugs lounge, sipping on dew,
As beetles play hide-and-seek too.
"Life above is such a circus show!"
They laugh and twirl, relishing the glow.

With laughter echoing in the soil,
They embrace the joy, the simple toil.
In the cradle, life bustles and thrives,
Under the layers, the humor survives.

Beneath the Weight of Time

In the depths, there's a party ongoing,
Time moves slow, yet laughter keeps flowing.
Old tree roots recall the silly strife,
"Remember the day we toppled that life?"

Raccoons wear hats made from fallen leaves,
As they plot pranks beneath ancient eaves.
They toast to the past with a nugget of joy,
Every laugh shared, a timeless employ.

Moles bring snacks from their dark little halls,
While shadows play tricks with giggly brawls.
"Who knew the ground was such a delight?"
With each hearty chortle, they light up the night.

So come down low, where the fun times are,
Where each whisper echoes like a distant star.
For beneath the weight of the ages gone,
The laughter of life carries on and on.

The Glow of Hidden Growth

Underneath where no one would guess,
Sprouts are giggling in colorful dress.
"I can't believe we're stuck in this clay!"
Said a cheeky sprout on a sunny day.

Wiggly roots throw a wild feast,
"More compost! Don't stop, let's increase!"
With worm smiles beaming, they dance around,
In their little world, happiness abounds.

With laughter that tickles the private soil,
They cultivate joy through every toil.
"Let's break the surface, cause a ruckus!"
A kaleidoscope of fun, they can trust.

So next time you peek at the earth so brown,
Remember the party that wears a green crown.
Below the surface, where mirth has a home,
Life's funny charm continues to roam.

The Soft Undercurrent

In a garden full of glee,
The weeds throw quite a spree.
They giggle soft as they creep,
Their nighttime secrets they keep.

They plant their tricks all around,
In their subterranean mound.
Jokes are cracked in the dirt,
While flowers laugh and smirk.

The carrots wear a leafy hat,
As earthworms dance, imagine that!
Beneath the ground, they whirl and twirl,
While butterflies above just swirl.

So next time you take a glance,
Remember there's a hidden dance.
Underneath the plants' sweet face,
Is a party space, a rooty place!

Life Anchored Deep

In the soil, a beetroot dreams,
Hatching out its crazy schemes.
"Let's hold a party," it squeaks,
While broccoli rolls and peeks.

Potatoes groove in the dark,
Planning their next weird quirk.
"Let's be mashed or fried," they say,
Delighting in their earthy play.

With every sprout and leafy cheer,
The hidden laughter draws near.
Anchored deep, where no one gazes,
They share their jokes and silly phrases.

So when you munch on that green,
Remember all the fun unseen.
Beneath the ground, life's just a blast,
With roots that throw a party vast!

The Invisible Ties

In the dark where secrets lie,
Potatoes pass the time nearby.
"What about a game of hide?"
They chuckle low with hidden pride.

Carrots compete to grow the most,
While radishes join the funny boast.
Ties that cannot be untied,
Their playful antics can't be denied.

The silly rhubarb tries to sing,
In its leafy cap of spring.
All the veggies share a wink,
As they chat and double think.

In a patch unseen, they shine,
Invisible friends by design.
So when you see that fresh-cut view,
Know there's laughter, just for you!

Murmurs from Below

Listen close, there's laughter near,
From the roots that share their cheer.
Murmurs bubble, soft and low,
In their little dirt-filled show.

"There's a turnip!" one might gasp,
"Dare we pull it, just to clasp?"
But the onion, wise and old,
Hands out laughs, no need to scold.

They play charades and crack a pun,
Shadows dancing, oh what fun!
Above, folks munch without a clue,
Of the merry world just a few.

Though we don't see their nightly prance,
They pull us in with every chance.
So when you taste that garden fare,
Just know there's chuckles everywhere!

The Labyrinth Below

In the depths where the gophers play,
A maze of tunnels leads astray.
Their snickers echo, a cheeky jest,
Digging contests? They're the best!

With rulers made of twigs and leaves,
Squirrels plot, with sticky weaves.
Who would win this underground race?
A sleepy tortoise? A speedy mouse face?

Down below, where shadows creep,
Spiders weave secrets, never asleep.
"Not a web, it's an art!" they boast,
While ants line up, their marching toast.

A party planned with a twist of fate,
Throw in some cheese, now that's first rate!
Underneath, they dance and sway,
In the labyrinth, let's all play!

Subterranean Stories

In the earth where the worms write prose,
Tales of treasures and silly clothes.
A mole, with glasses, reads aloud,
The audience? Just a very proud crowd.

Rabbits gossip in fluffy circles,
About a fox with questionable burbles.
"What's his secret, does he even try?"
They giggle hard, beneath the sky.

A raccoon with a hat made of leaves,
Swears he's seen the craziest thieves.
His buddy the badger rolls his eyes,
"Some just like singing, to my surprise!"

Each tale told brings laughter near,
Beneath the soil, joys are clear.
A world of whimsy, secretly spun,
In the deep, where they all have fun!

Guardians of the Underbelly

A hedgehog dons a crown of twigs,
"Bow to me," he winks, doing jigs.
Guardians they are, of this underground place,
Where mushrooms dance with all their grace.

A gopher general leads the pack,
With a carrot sword, ready to attack!
"Hold on tight!" shrieks a brave little beetle,
As thunder rolls, oh what a sequel!

Mock battles fill the quiet air,
Where laughter looms, without a care.
"Trolls aren't real!" squeaks a tiny mouse,
But down here, they're cooler than any house.

So they frolic and twirl in the damp,
Living life like a wild romp and stamp.
Guardians together, full of good cheer,
In the underbelly, we've no fear!

The Silent Tether

Beneath the grass, they pull and tug,
A world misplaced, still full of mug.
"Play hide and seek!" shouts a lively ant,
"Just remember, no need to chant!"

A thread of laughter binds them tight,
As roots of whispers ignite the night.
The worms plot a surprise at dawn,
In this wacky land, mischief's never gone.

"Who stole my lunch?" asks a frantic snail,
As they scatter, leaving a glittering trail.
The answer's simple, a wise old crow,
"Just follow the giggles; they always glow!"

Down below, where the fun keeps growing,
Friends gather 'round, the energy flowing.
With each jest shared, a bond appears,
In the silent tether, laughter steers.

Harmony in the Dark

In the garden where shadows play,
Bunnies dance and mischief sway.
The gnomes gossip, holding cups,
While ants negotiate their way up.

Twilight giggles, crickets sing,
A moonbeam pranks, a playful fling.
Squirrels reenact the heist of nuts,
As owls judge from their cozy ruts.

Beneath the soil, a party brews,
With worms in hats and roots in shoes.
The fox laughs as he takes a peek,
At the ruckus that makes the night unique.

So when it's dark, don't disbelieve,
There's a carnival hiding up the sleeve.
Join the madness, don't miss the jest,
Where life underground is at its best!

The Quiet Interlace

In a land where giggles grow,
A hedgehog juggles—don't be slow!
A snail in shades claims it's a race,
While moles plan their secret base.

Underneath, the whispers reel,
A band of roots in a funny wheel.
The mushrooms twirl, wear tiny hats,
While beetles compete in acrobats.

A worm slide down a leafy slide,
Waving to the bumblebee pride.
"Catch me if you can!" he squeaks with glee,
But grass blades giggle, "You'll never be free."

In this layer of chuckles dim,
Where laughter blooms and lights grow grim.
If you dare to peek past the ground,
Funny treasures are waiting to be found!

Beneath Starlit Layers

At the stroke of midnight's glance,
Centipedes are out for a dance.
Fireflies sprinkle the dark, oh my!
As critters in tuxedos pass by.

A family of roots play charades,
While raccoons wear outlandish spades.
Junipers hum a catchy tune,
As laughter echoes beneath the moon.

A badger busts out his best moves,
While a hedgehog plays DJ grooves.
"Shake it, shake it!" the stars declare,
As the earth spins with a cheeky flair.

In this underground soirée's cheer,
All creatures unite, sipping root beer.
For parties bloom where the sun won't creep,
In the cozy caverns, secrets keep!

The Lattice of Existence

In a patch where wiggles meet,
Worms huddle up for a day of heat.
A flower's hat goes slightly askew,
As beetles argue about their due.

A dandelion dreams of the sky,
While munching on the clouds that pass by.
"Are we lost?" it asks with a grin,
As the roots nod with a cheeky spin.

Hidden gems dance in the mire,
Singing loudly like they're on fire.
Where mushrooms cheer in jubilation,
While frogs start a croaky vacation.

So dig a little where the fun is real,
In this matrix where laughter's the meal.
For the story goes deep, not in the light,
But in giggles and chuckles all through the night!

Secrets in the Soil

In a garden, secrets hide,
Worms party with pride.
They chuckle and cheer,
While my veggies appear!

A carrot's a spy, so sleek,
With a top hat, how unique!
The radishes gossip away,
'The turnips eat cake, what a day!'

Moles playing cards underground,
With no sound, just a mound.
They shuffle and deal,
Beneath our squeaky heel!

Potatoes have dreams, quite absurd,
They want to fly, that's the word.
Yet here they must grow,
In soil, not in a show!

Tangles of Time

Through tangled vines that twist and wind,
Old tales of veggies, one can find.
A cucumber once wore a suit,
And thought it was quite classy, to boot!

Beets tell stories of days so bright,
When they danced under the moonlight.
They loved to prance, oh what a sight,
Their rhythm, a rooty delight!

The radish rolled its eyes with flair,
While the zucchini combed its hair.
They shared a laugh, a fun trot,
All underground, in a joyful spot.

Yet time rolls on, as roots confide,
In shadows where giggles abide.
They carry dreams with silent glee,
In this crazy underground jubilee!

Silent Depths

In silent depths where whispers stray,
The potatoes plot their great decay.
'Tomorrow,' they say, 'let's prank the sun,'
With shadows and dirt, oh, it'll be fun!

Carrots can't wait for veggie day,
Where they chase light and laugh at clay.
But when frolics come to a pause,
They dig in deep and plot with cause!

Scarecrows ignore the buzz below,
While mushrooms host a show, you know!
In silence they share a hearty snack,
With roots and laughs, there's no lack!

Yet through the cracks above so bright,
They toss out punchlines, sheer delight.
In silent depths, their laughter echoes,
With earthy jokes, the fun only grows!

Echoes of the Underground

Down where the creatures take their seat,
Echoes of laughter, quite a treat.
The mushroom jokes never fall flat,
They giggle and roll, imagine that!

A snail plays music, slow and smooth,
To entertain roots, with every groove.
'This beat's been growing since fifty-three!'
Chortled the beet, joyous and free.

Rabbits listen and nod their heads,
As the radish legends flow like threads.
'The cabbage, once brave, chased off a crow!'
They snicker and chuckle at the show.

In the echoing dark, tales entwine,
With roots as the stars, they brightly shine.
Beneath the world so loud above,
They share their quirks, all born of love!

Secrets Buried Deep

In the garden, gnomes all laugh,
As they tell jokes on grass's half.
Worms giggle under leafy sheets,
While ants throw parties with tiny treats.

A shovel's quest uncovers cheer,
Mice in top hats drink root beer.
The daisies dance like it's their fate,
To throw a bash and celebrate.

Underneath, where mischief swirls,
Squirrels plot and twirl like girls.
Their plans are wacky, full of flair,
While sneaky raccoons steal their share.

So many secrets hide with glee,
The soil's laughter, wild and free.
Dig a bit and take a peek,
You might find nuts that chirp and speak!

Silent Currents

Fish in the stream share whispered tales,
Of mermaids who wear shimmering veils.
The rocks sit still, though they are sly,
Plotting pranks while the frogs hop by.

Under the bridge, the secrets swap,
The turtles laugh, 'Do we ever stop?'
They get tickled by drifting leaves,
And joke about a world that believes.

Drifting dreams, where shadows hide,
Playful splashes come and glide.
Bubbles rise with stories grand,
As the minnows start a band.

With tiny tunes and whimsical sounds,
The current holds its giggling rounds.
Join the concert, grab a seat,
For nature's laughter is quite the treat!

Forgotten Touchstones

Beneath the stones, a party brews,
Where crickets wear colorful shoes.
Gilly the grasshopper leads the throng,
As ants hum their favorite song.

Forgotten coins from ages past,
Drink dew drop drinks and have a blast.
The giggles echo through the grass,
While sleepy badgers sneak and pass.

Ticklish roots tickle all around,
As secrets whisper from the ground.
The daisies nod, they can't resist,
Each hidden flower has a twist.

Through muffled laughter, stories weave,
A world beneath no one would believe.
So if you stumble on a patch,
Listen closely, there's quite a catch!

Echoes of the Subterranean

Down below where shadows dwell,
The critters plot and cast their spell.
A hedgehog juggles, and we all cheer,
While moles duck away from all the jeer.

In tunnels snug, the echoes play,
As fireflies dance at end of day.
With tiny hats and twinkling eyes,
Their laughter sparkles like the skies.

The roots hold tapestries of fun,
As earthworms run a marathon.
"Squirm faster!" hollers the cheering crew,
In the underworld of the slightly askew.

So drop your worries, chuckle loud,
For in the dark, we form a crowd.
With echoes bouncing, come take part,
In the laughter woven from the heart!

Between the Layers of Life

In the soil where veggies play,
Carrots giggle, 'Hey, look our way!'
Potatoes are hiding with silly grins,
While turnips dance in their vegetable skins.

Underneath where secrets hide,
Radishes roll like they've got pride,
Beets in burrows with colors bright,
While lettuce laughs under the moonlight.

In this garden, a party unfolds,
With worms as DJs, spinning gold,
Compost piles whisper jokes and lore,
As daffodils wave, eager for more!

So when you munch on veggies raw,
Remember their humor, their silly law,
For life underground is a whimsical race,
In layers where laughter finds its place.

The Subtle Pulse of Existence

Beneath the ground, a chatter does swell,
Crickets tell tales that you'd never tell,
Mice debate whether cheese is divine,
While earthworms sip on their home-brewed wine.

Twitching roots tell funny jokes in the dark,
As ants hold auditions, each looking to spark,
A dance-off to celebrate all things earthy,
Where fungi offer their best, oh so quirky!

A dandelion dreams of being a queen,
Yet down below, it's a real-life machine,
Playing hide and seek with thesaurus weeds,
As beetles make puns in their leafy creeds.

So if you kneel and give them a listen,
You might just hear the ground's funny vision,
In the pulse of the earth, life takes its chance,
With giggles and wiggles, it joins the dance.

Hidden Whispers

In the depths where chuckles collide,
Mushrooms whisper, 'Oh, what a ride!'
Toadstools giggle at squirrels' fine tricks,
While snails share stories with little quick clicks.

A dandelion's snooze is a quest for a friend,
As worms host parties that never quite end,
Fungus in bright hats serves the best of the stew,
While creepy-crawlies do the conga for two!

The ants bring the snacks in a parade of delight,
Picnicking under roots, oh, what a sight!
With soil's own humor and laughter galore,
Join the fun, dig deep, and explore!

For life underground, so lively and spry,
Has secrets that giggle and winks from the sky,
If you dare to listen, you'll hear the cheer,
In hidden whispers, life's humor is clear.

The Veil of Earth

Beneath the crust, a party is brewing,
With moles and gophers, the laughter is spewing!
The dirt breeds jesters with roots as their friends,
Telling tall tales that never quite ends.

A gopher juggles with acorns galore,
While beetles host karaoke and roar,
In a world where the petals delightfully spin,
The mud cakes their faces like pure, silly kin.

Worms wear their hats, oh so proudly askew,
As grass blades shimmy with a fresh morning dew,
Down in the dark, it's a fanciful place,
A comedy club with no hint of grace!

So when you feel dirt 'neath your feet start to sway,
Remember the laughter, the fun on display,
For beneath this surface lies more than we see,
Just a gathering of giggles, so joyful and free.

Quiet Bonds

In the garden, whispers fly,
Earthworms giggle as they pass by.
Mice debate what snacks to steal,
While ants plan feasts that make us squeal.

Underneath the grass they plot,
A secret world where it's all hot.
Beetles dance in evening light,
Creating chaos, pure delight.

The snails take bets on who goes fast,
Frogs cheer loudly, hoping for a blast.
With each little poke and every tease,
Life's a game, played with such ease.

So while we bask up on the ground,
Beneath us, joy is all around.
A party rages, quite absurd,
In the quiet space where none have heard.

Underworld Symphony

Down below where shadows play,
Worms compose their cabaret.
A piano made of stones they sing,
Celebrating every little thing.

Moles tap dance, their hats askew,
While crickets join to form a crew.
Each note a jest, each beat a laugh,
Nature's charm, a witty gaffe.

The roots sway to the jazzy beat,
Raccoons sneak in for a little treat.
A burrowed stage, a dome of earth,
Where every critter finds its worth.

With night's curtain, the show begins,
Under the stars, the mischief spins.
In harmony, they twist and twine,
This underground, a place divine.

Nature's Hidden Symphony

Underneath where shadows dwell,
The murmurs of the ground do tell.
Beetles strum their tiny strings,
While nature surely laughs and sings.

A chubby toad croaks out a tune,
In the moonlight, here's the rune.
Grass blades sway, a gentle dance,
As squirrels twirl in merry prance.

The soil hums, a funky beat,
Beneath our feet, life's quite a treat.
Dancing roots in rhythmic lines,
Creating laughter in sunny shrines.

So if you listen, take a chance,
You might hear them sing and prance.
A symphony you'll never grasp,
Yet smiles linger in each gasp.

The Heart of the Earth

Deep in the ground, a secret hide,
Where gophers wear their heels with pride.
They tell stories of the days gone by,
While ladybugs gently sigh.

Under the dirt, a playful bustle,
Creatures gather with a little tussle.
The busy ants throw a surprise,
A birthday bash in a mole's disguise.

Mushrooms serve as tables set,
For all the laughter you can bet.
With roots like dancers, swirling round,
In a festival beneath the ground.

So let us cheer for those below,
Who spin the tales we do not know.
The heart of Earth beats loud and clear,
In every giggle, in every cheer.

Spirit Below

In the garden where the gnomes dwell,
The wild carrots plot and yell.
They rave about the things they grow,
While giggling deep where no one goes.

The worms have formed a rock band crew,
With melodies that make you blue.
They dance among the underground mess,
Creating chaos, I must confess.

Moles wear sunglasses, digging in vain,
While splashing through the mud and rain.
They dig up treasure, or so they claim,
But mostly just their blushing shame.

In this world where laughter reigns,
The spirits tease, forgetting pains.
Their jokes are silly, never deep,
As they play hide and seek in heaps.

The Depths of Belonging

Down below, where the shadows tease,
The ants throw parties, all with ease.
They shuffle past, in lines so neat,
While arguing about their favorite beet.

The snails debate on who is fast,
While rolling their thoughts from the past.
Each shell a home, but quite a sight,
As they slip and slide – oh what a fight!

The critters whisper, "Who came where?"
While clutching snacks, or maybe air.
With giggles echoing like a drum,
They celebrate their nighttime fun.

In tunnels thick with tales galore,
They sing about adventures more.
In every nook, a chuckle thrives,
Underground, where humor survives.

The Tender Grip

In the soil where secrets lie,
The radishes wave their leafy high.
With tales of sprouting, they start to boast,
Who knew they'd make such charming hosts?

Carrots play peek-a-boo with glee,
While telling stories just for me.
They joke about their muddy plight,
And laugh at every garden fight.

Above ground, the squirrels make a fuss,
Thinking their acorns are fabulous.
But down below, the chatter swells,
As veggies spin their funny tales.

The garden thrives in sweet delight,
With roots entwined, a funny sight.
And in this dance beneath the fray,
The laughter grows, it's here to stay.

Shadows of Our History

In the depths where whispers bloom,
The crickets croon like a late-night tune.
They share the gossip of days gone past,
As the soil snickers, holding fast.

The beetles argue who should rule,
While dreaming of the old school.
Their tales entwined with ancient jest,
In this world of worms, we're all guests.

The mushrooms giggle, feeling fine,
As they sip on dew like it's fine wine.
With every drop, stories unfold,
Of mischief and fun from years of old.

In shadows cast by time's embrace,
They celebrate their quirky place.
A history rich, both brave and sweet,
Where laughter and soil always meet.

Under the Surface

In the garden, gnomes do sneer,
Laughing at the worms that cheer.
Underneath the leafy crown,
Secret parties goin' down!

Frogs in tuxedos, sipping grass,
Toadstool stools for all, alas!
Moles play cards and dig for gold,
While the daisies dance, oh so bold!

Squirrels swing on hidden vines,
Planning mischief 'neath the pines.
The root world's wild; it's quite the scene,
Where even rocks might join the routine!

So if you peek beneath the soil,
You'll find us laughing, plotting toil.
Not just dirt but giggles thrive,
Where lowdown delights really come alive!

Unraveled Mysteries

Beneath the bed, where dust bunnies skate,
A treasure map, or maybe just fate!
Unclaimed socks throw a party each night,
While a lint monster gives them a fright!

Vermin play poker behind the wall,
In a secret club with high stakes, y'all!
A cheese wheel whispers tales so grand,
Of daring escapes and pizza band!

A lost remote sits back in glee,
With old coins, and a recipe!
What's hidden down there? Oh, what a spree,
Banana peels laughing, wild and free!

So if you wander, spare a glance,
The unseen world has quite a dance.
Mysteries play while humans snooze,
In the realm where no one can refuse!

Unseen Lifelines

In the kitchen, a brave potato spies,
Sassier than a carrot, oh what a surprise!
They hold below their veggie parade,
Witty whispers that never fade!

Tomatoes gossip in shades of red,
About peas that dream of being fed.
The celery's strutting in stylish flair,
While garlic's breath gives all a scare!

Roots and veggies, united by fate,
Hold a conference on the dinner plate.
"Let's spice it up!" the onions shout,
With laughter echoing all about!

So as you munch on crunchy bliss,
Remember the wisdom you might miss.
The lifelines that stretch and twist through time,
Have jokes and games, all in their prime!

The Depth of Sentiments

Down below, where the giggles bloom,
Life's little secrets create a room.
In the shadows, friendships brew,
With puns so wild, they slip and skew!

Beneath the grass, a band resides,
Playing tunes while everyone hides.
A conga line of critters sways,
Unraveling laughter in sneaky ways!

The depths are rich with joy untold,
Where snails in disco seem quite bold.
With all their glitter, they schmooze and prance,
In a circle of slime, they take their chance!

So when you think of what's below,
Remember the smiles that happen to flow.
For underneath our feet so fine,
The comedy thrives, like aged fine wine!

Beneath the Quiet Ground

Worms are throwing parties, oh what a sight,
Dancing in the dark, beneath moonlight.
The soil's a disco, with roots in the groove,
Shuffle along, they've got nothing to prove.

Moles tell jokes, they're quite the comedians,
Nibbling on snacks, like true vegetarians.
While ants bring the drinks, in tiny red cups,
Under the surface, the fun never erupts.

Traces of Ancestors

If you dig down deep, you might just find,
Great-great-grandpa's mustache, a relic combined.
His barber was a beetle, so sharp and so slick,
Chopping off grass like a seasoned old trick.

A history in dirt, who knew it could be,
Potsherds and acorns, like a crazy spree.
Grandma's old recipes, served on a leaf,
With laughter and wit, a great leafy relief.

The Undergrowth Chronicles

Here beneath the trees, there's gossip abound,
Squirrels squawk tales that are truly profound.
The shadows wave high-fives in grassy delight,
While poets of the underground battle all night.

Chipmunks recite sonnets, no clue what they mean,
In the theater of roots, which is quite the scene.
Fungi tap dance, in a moldy ballet,
Nature's own circus, come watch if you may!

Life's Veins: A Silent History

Beneath the green canvas, life stitches its fun,
With fibers that giggle, never on the run.
In pools of muddy laughter, the earth comes alive,
Gnarled roots throw shade, while critters survive.

Life's got its secrets, made of clay and of grime,
Roots stretch into legends, but they take their time.
Beneath the loud surface, there's silence and cheer,
In the dance of the dandelions, there's nothing to fear.

Stories Written in the Dark

In the garden a squirrel plots,
Stealing seeds from the flower pots.
While worms wag tails with a grin,
Whispering tales of where they've been.

The moon giggles, casting a glow,
On secrets that only the night can know.
A beetle on a mission to brag,
Rides a leaf like a speedy flag.

Crickets chirp a soft serenade,
While shadows dance in the cool parade.
They all conspire, hatching a scheme,
In the dark, it's a funny dream.

So when you step into the night,
Listen close, there's humor in sight.
For even earth has laughter crude,
In its stories, fits for a brood.

Echoes of Life Below

Down below, where the critters play,
A parade of ants on their busy way.
They march in lines, so neat and spry,
As one trips over a worm nearby.

Fungi giggle, in vibrant hues,
Throwing parties, sharing their views.
Mice share rumors, all ear to ear,
The soil has tales that tickle the ear.

Beneath the grass, there's a ruckus loud,
With moles debating who's the wisest crowd.
The roots are vibing to their own tune,
As gophers dance under the watchful moon.

Each echo a chuckle from the ground,
Life below offers laughter profound.
In the depth, where the mischief brews,
There's joy in the tales, and that one's true.

The Underground Woven Dreams

In a world made of dirt and clay,
Where raccoons plot and laugh all day,
The mouse tailors hats for the snails,
While fireflies narrate epic tales.

A spider spins webs, not for fright,
But to catch giggles on starry nights.
Singing worms strum on the soil's strings,
Each note a joy, as the dark night sings.

Rabbits wear shades in their burrowed nook,
Reading the news from an underground book.
Together they scheme a funny caper,
Whispers of mischief, none dare to taper.

So if you wander to where the roots sprout,
Listen for chuckles, hear all about.
For down below, where dreams take flight,
The humor blooms, hidden from sight.

Deep Conversations of the Earth

Down in the depths, roots laugh and tease,
Sharing their gossip with buzz and breeze.
Worms debate about who digs the best,
While rocks sit back, quietly blessed.

The ants compare their building skills,
Trading tall tales that give us thrills.
A spirited chat, with giggles abound,
Bringing life to the underground ground.

Moles spy on the fun, shaking their heads,
While critters make beds from leaves and threads.
The earth is alive with merriment grand,
As every creature lends a hand.

So when the grass rolls over your feet,
Remember there's humor where groundlings meet.
For in the soil, where laughs emerge,
Life's deep conversations always surge.

The Depths of Kinship

In the cellar, Aunt Mabel's jam,
Sits beside Uncle Joe's old spam.
We laugh and share our family tales,
Of cousins lost and epic fails.

Grandpa's jokes still make us groan,
A twisted tale of hair, now grown.
With every laugh, our bond's renewed,
In this odd mix, we find our dude.

The family tree has some weird fruit,
A festival of quirks, absolute.
We dance around, our spirits bright,
In the cellar, shared with pure delight.

So raise a glass to roots unknown,
In laughter's light, we all have grown.
The depths of fam bring joy and cheer,
A crazy bunch, yet oh so dear.

Sprouts of Memory

In Grandma's garden, weeds rejoice,
She fights them off with her loud voice.
Remember that time when flowers fled?
We chased them down, had a good thread.

Each sprout holds tales of mischief past,
Like the beans that climbed the fence too fast.
"Why do they run?" we used to muse,
Maybe they heard of Grandma's shoes!

With gales of laughter, we plant anew,
A veggie patch where joy just grew.
Our harvest's a mix of smiles and tears,
Funny how time flies through the years.

So here's to veggies and memories sweet,
With every bite, laughter's our treat.
We've got a garden, wild and nutty,
Sprouts of joy, oh ain't that funny?

Life Among the Shadows

In the attic, dust bunnies reign,
With old toys that bear the strain.
We laugh at the highs and silly lows,
While dodging what the old cat knows.

Shadows dance, the light does flee,
A ghost of Dad, who drank too much tea.
He'll tell a tale then disappear,
Leaving behind his wobbly cheer.

The cobwebs weave a story grand,
Of hidden finds, both strange and bland.
Each treasure chest a laugh-ensued,
Life's oddities perpetually brewed.

In shades we find our family bliss,
With every ghostly tale that's amiss.
The attic's chaos is where we play,
In life's shadows, we find our way.

Shadows of Connection

In the park where shadows meet,
We share our snacks, a strange little treat.
"Is that a sandwich or a shoe?"
Laughing together, there's work to do.

Friends like roots sprawled out wide,
In the picnic chaos, we take pride.
Mismatched socks on everyone here,
A fashion statement, loud and clear.

Side by side, we plant our jokes,
Twisting tales of silly hoaxes.
With every laugh and jest we sow,
Shadows of kinship start to grow.

So join the fun beneath the boughs,
In this madness, we take our vows.
Friendship's a salad, quirky and wild,
Shadows united, forever beguiled.

Hidden Synapses

Beneath the ground, where worms conspire,
Whispers travel, through muck and mire.
If soil could talk, it'd tell a joke,
About a potato that learned to poke.

Hiding treasures in pots of clay,
A carrot's dream to dance one day.
The radishes giggle, buried in beds,
While moles are planning their covert spreads.

Silly fungi share secrets in glee,
Trading gossip like it's high tea.
With a chuckle, the daisies bloom,
While their roots plot mischief, plotting doom.

So here's to the antics below our feet,
Where dirt is filled with laughter sweet.
The underground club, where all things meet,
A wacky world, where life is neat!

Nature's Silent Veins

In the dark, where the giggles grow,
Squirrels plot, they steal the show.
Mushrooms dance like it's a fest,
While beetles jest at their own behest.

The secret lives of roots in stealth,
Whispers traded for hidden wealth.
While trees share stories, leaf by leaf,
A comedy show, beyond belief.

Earthworms worm their way in lines,
Making paths like silly designs.
With a twist and a sock, they turn and tumble,
Underneath the surface, while we all grumble.

Let's raise a toast to the underground,
Where nature's laughter can be found.
In silent veins, the jokes are played,
A hilarious mess that has never frayed!

The Language of Earth

Beneath the grass, it's quite absurd,
Rabbits writing their own word.
A clod of dirt with tales to tell,
Of garden antics, oh so swell!

Moles with microphones, ready to croon,
What's happening with the coming moon?
Sprouts gossiping on a sunny day,
Trading banter in their own way.

The pebbles chuckle in cheeky tone,
Sharing puns when we're all alone.
While roots hum softly, a giggly sound,
In their silly world, we're all spellbound.

So listen in, to the earth's slight grin,
With laughter bubbling from deep within.
The language of life that we ignore,
Is giggly nonsense and so much more!

Resilient Threads

In the depths of dirt, where critters play,
Laughter bubbles up to greet the day.
With resilient threads that weave a dance,
A mischief-making scene at every chance.

The daisies train in synchronized moves,
While the grass hums beats in earthy grooves.
Ants with tiny top hats march in line,
Debugging paths that somehow align.

Roots throwing shade, while they pull a prank,
Beneath the surface, they've got a bank.
Trading secrets with the gophers near,
Where laughter echoes, drawing us near.

So let's giggle at nature's parade,
With all the antics that life has made.
In threads of resilience, joy takes flight,
As they tickle the earth with pure delight!

The Tapestry of Earth

Beneath the ground where critters play,
A hidden world hums night and day.
Worms throw parties, mice bring cheese,
While old stones gossip with the breeze.

The daisies dance, the moles dig deep,
As earthworms plot, and mushrooms leap.
Cabbages join in, all dressed up fine,
Throwing down roots, sipping on brine.

A toothy grin from a radish bright,
Says, "Let's have fun, from morning to night!"
The carrots laugh in their orange garb,
While beets tell jokes that make you charred.

So here's to the soil, so rich and absurd,
In this underground club, everyone's heard.
Where laughter echoes, and roots intertwine,
The tapestry thickens, divine and benign.

Unwritten Chronicles

In the soil, a tale unfolds,
Chanting secrets the earth beholds.
A gopher's diary still unwritten,
Filled with mischief, adventures smitten.

Potatoes think they run the show,
With tales of treasures, and tricks to throw.
While onions cry, for all to see,
Their layered lives are filled with glee.

The squirrels twist plots in the shade,
Climbing trees while playing charades.
Bees write sonnets on a petal's face,
Their buzzing rhythm gives the chase.

So let's uncover all that dirt,
The stories told and those that hurt.
In an epic saga of humor bright,
The chronicles wait for the day and night.

Celestial Threads Below

Stars twinkle high, but look down low,
There's a party, and the fun's aglow!
Rabbits moonwalk with shovels in hand,
While fireflies dance in a grand band.

Wiggly beings weave laughs so fine,
As roots twine tightly like a jumping vine.
Celestial threads in the earth arise,
With every chuckle reaching the skies.

Radishes sport their hats of green,
Making jokes that are quite obscene.
While grubby gnomes throw spirited darts,
Down here, it's a riot of clever arts.

So here's to the rift where the fun resides,
Where every squirming giggle abides.
Beneath our feet, the universe sings,
With witty earthlings and silly things.

The Weight of Ancestors

Beneath the soil, the giants rest,
With roots like stories, they are the best.
Old sprouts chuckle, with tales to share,
About how to dance without a care.

Nuts and seeds with epic flair,
Argue over who's got the best hair.
While mushrooms gossip about their dreams,
In a world stitched with laughter it seems.

Ancestors bold whisper from below,
With tips on how to steal the show.
But ferns just smirk, saying, "Hey, look here,
We're the cool ones, let's give a cheer!"

So let's remember those in the past,
Who giggled and thrived, and always had a blast.
With the weight of their joy pushing up high,
We'll dance in the sunlight and laugh 'til we cry.

Echoes of Forgotten Growth

In the garden of giggles and weeds,
A carrot once danced, fulfilling its needs.
It wore a top hat, so odd and so bright,
Pretending to be a magician at night.

A radish then laughed, rolled on the grass,
Claiming it once was a star of the class.
They held a debate on whose roots were best,
While the lettuce leaf snoozed, taking a rest.

Pumpkins told tales of their grandest parade,
How they zipped down the lane, unafraid.
But buried below, in the dirt they all stayed,
Just munching on snacks, getting ever more swayed.

In this world of layers underground, so sly,
The beets start to bubble and whisper, oh my!
With secrets and stories that nobody knows,
It's a party of veggies that nobody shows.

Hidden Threads of Life

Beneath the grass where the critters conspire,
The ants hold a meeting, plans to retire.
They gossip of leaves and the woes of the sky,
While the worms make a bet on who'll grow wings to fly.

One day a mole, with a hat made of cheese,
Stumbled into a party, surprised by the breeze.
He wiggled and giggled, a sight oh so rare,
While roots peeked around with curious flair.

The onions, all teary, sang songs of regret,
Hoping for sunshine to lighten the fret.
While the clovers would chuckle, "What's that on your face?"
"Just my layers of charm!" they proclaimed with grace.

In the maze down below, where the laughs dance and weave,
Life's a carnival ride that's hard to believe.
With roots intertwined and jokes never stale,
The underground circus, a comedic tale.

Unseen Journeys Below

In the depths where the dark and the silly collide,
A potato once took an underground ride.
It wore a bowtie made of freshly grown thyme,
Claiming its journey was truly sublime.

Around it there swayed, a troupe of young sprouts,
Whispering secrets, chuckling, no doubts.
"I swear I just saw a ghostly vine dance,
It twirled like a ballerina, given a chance!"

The carrots cheered louder, "Let's form a band!
Who can beat our beats, on this fertile land?"
The turnips just snickered, "You call that a groove?
Wait till you see how the celery moves!"

Together they giggled, in grand harmony,
Making melodies down where no one could see.
In their hidden domain, such joy to explore,
Underneath laughter, life hums evermore.

The Tapestry of Hidden Networks

Underfoot lies a realm where the chuckles are rife,
Where mushrooms debate about the meaning of life.
One said, "I'm a poet, my rhymes are divine!"
While others clapped softly, "Have you tried the wine?"

The dandelions, bold, took a stand with a cheer,
"Let's toast to the roots, to laughter, to beer!"
While the thistles lamented their prickly designs,
Saying, "We're the punchline of nature's fine lines!"

In the nets of the soil, with humor so slick,
Worms spun tall tales of their escapade trips.
"Did you hear about Bob, who dug just too deep,
A raccoon stole his hat! Now it's his grief."

Thus life runs hilariously, unseen yet profound,
Where the jests of the greenery flourish unbound.
In this tapestry woven from laughter and grace,
There's comedy blooming in each special place.

Whispers from the Earth

Under the ground where the gophers play,
The earthworms wiggle in a funny way.
Moles throw parties in their underground spots,
And laugh at the veggies they've stolen from plots.

Beneath the soil, it's a wild affair,
Squirrels gossip about the seeds they share.
Bugs do the cha-cha, ants dance in lines,
While roots sip tea with their leafy designs.

Hidden away, the potatoes joke,
"Tell us again about that giant bloke!"
The carrots snicker with a twinkle in eyes,
As the radishes whisper of monster-sized fries.

In this quirky world without a sunbeam,
Life is a riot, like a madcap dream.
So if you dig deep, you just might find,
Laughter and giggles of a very odd kind.

Secrets of the Subterranean

The gophers speak in whispers and squeaks,
Trading their secrets, so slyly it peaks.
They fashion a world where the dirt is their gold,
While worms tell tales that are wiggly and bold.

Down in the dark, the mushrooms convene,
With fungi gossip, a curious scene.
"Did you see what the roots pulled off last night?"
"Sure did! It was a fungi delight!"

Within the depths, they craft their parade,
With beetles adorned in their bug-friendly raid.
Laughter erupts over acorn cap jokes,
While the soil erupts in fits of real pokes.

So if you perceive a soft giggle or two,
It's just the critters sharing old news.
In the underground's embrace, full of cheer,
Lurks joy and mischief, all hidden down here.

The Veins of Silence

In the silence where the clovers dance,
Worms create beats to a secret romance.
"Did you hear about that tree with the bark?"
"It's a real showstopper, even in dark!"

Beneath the noise of the bustling above,
The critters all gather, sharing their love.
With roots intertwined in a dance of delight,
They throw a shindig every late night.

The grubs tell stories of past garden woes,
While ants debate on the best picnic shows.
"Last week I found a crumb the size of my head!"
It's a banquet of laughter, where everyone's fed.

So lean down and listen to what they say,
For merriment thrives in the underground play.
Amidst the soil's heart, nestled snugly and wide,
The laughter of life constantly resides.

Shadows in the Soil

In shadows where mischief and fun conspired,
Silly critters laugh, all whimsically wired.
The rocks hold court, with pebbles as jesters,
While worms do impressions of silly old testers.

Moles fashion hats from leaves and old threads,
Hosting a gala for all sorts of spreads.
"Who wore it best—the daisy or fern?"
In this droll assembly, what wonders we learn!

The ants throw picnics, the beetles take bets,
On who makes the best of their veggie-shaped sets.
"Last time I served it, I'm sure it was great!"
But still, to this day, they're debating that plate.

So dive in the ground, let your laughter abound,
For shimmering shadows hold joy all around.
The earth has a party, you should join the spree,
The echoes of laughter, they're waiting for thee.

Guardians of the Undersoil

In the kingdom of mud, worms play king,
Ruling over secrets, they dance and sing.
A carrot's lost voice, in sweet protest,
'Why must I hide? I'm the underground best!'

The radish chuckles, a jester so round,
"Why do we dig when there's laughter above ground?"
With roots all entangled, they share a drink,
In a party of veggies, they giggle and wink.

The beets wear top hats, all fancy and bright,
Waving to mushrooms, their friends of the night.
"Don't mind the dirt! It's our favorite dress,
A squash full of puns, we laugh, no less!"

With a trowel and shovel, they plot and conspire,
To tickle the toes of the grass in the mire.
So next time you munch on a salad so fine,
Remember the jokes that grow down the line!

The Language of the Buried

Deep under the soil, a squirrel can hear,
The gossip of grasses whispering near.
"Did you see that?" says the root of a tree,
"Her bark's looking fabulous! Just wait, you'll see!"

The stones sit in silence, judging the jokes,
As weeds tell tall tales and giggle like folks.
"I heard that the sun sometimes comes down to play,"
Said a brave little flower in bright shades of gray.

"Mole comes with a shovel, he digs with such flair,
But lately, we suspect he's too stuck in his lair."
The compost, quite cheeky, says, "What's that in news?
A rumor of ferns trying on new shades of hues?"

So next time you wander above in the light,
Remember the laughter that echoes at night.
Beneath all the surface, the laughter and play,
Turns dirt into joy in the silliest way!

Visions in the Depths

In caverns of chaos, the moles wear a cape,
Using their minds to design a new shape.
"Why dig in circles? Let's try digging squares,
With angles and colors, we're moles with great flair!"

A beet says, "Stop! You're causing a stir,
Your wild underground dreams are making me purr!"
The mushrooms all giggle, saying with glee,
"Let's host a parade of the roots and the tree!"

With glittery glances from the deep loam below,
They plan a good time wearing hats made of dough.
"Let's dance, let's prance, for the gophers in town,
We'll throw them a party and spin them around!"

So don't be surprised, if you dig in your yard,
To find a big bash with the earth as a card.
They party so hard that the surface will quake,
All in the name of some roots and a shake!

The Lament of the Forgotten Woods

There once lived a branch that had dreams of its own,
"I'd like to be famous, not just overgrown!"
The leaves wisely scolded, "Stay rooted in place,
A tree with big dreams is a tree gone to space!"

A squirrel rolled by with a nut for its woes,
"Quit dreaming too hard, you'll forget how to grow!"
But the branch just chuckled, "Oh, isn't it neat?
To dream in the shade and to dance with my feet!"

A nesting bird laughed, "You're all bark and no bite,
But let's throw a party to celebrate fright!"
They swung from the branches and tickled the grass,
Shouted, "We're legends! Come join us en masse!"

So if you find yourself near woods in despair,
Just listen for giggles that float in the air.
For beneath all the woes, in the trees up above,
Are tales of the silly, of dreams, and of love!

Life in the Loam

In the dirt where worms reside,
A party's brewing deep inside.
Earth's secrets wiggle all around,
With every spade, more smiles found.

Moles in tuxedos dance with glee,
While ants serve snacks that taste like tea.
Beetles belt out their finest tunes,
Beneath the sun and laughing moons.

Playing hide and seek with roots,
Who knew they had such silly suits?
In loamy realms where giggles play,
Life's a jest that won't decay.

So dive on down, don't be a bore,
The underground's an open door.
With laughter sprouting from the ground,
Join the fun where joy is found.

Threads of the Past

In timeless soil, tales weave and twine,
Of veggies who dream of pasta divine.
Carrots brag about their orange hue,
While rhubarbs snicker, 'We're a treat too!'

Old potatoes claim they once were stars,
Who traveled from gardens to grand bazaars.
Peas gossip 'neath the leafy drape,
About a radish with a fanciful cape.

Underneath, the stories stack,
With every sprout, a cheeky quack.
Sweet potatoes boast of hidden flair,
While onions just tear up with despair.

So plant your tales among the seeds,
Where laughter grows and friendship breeds.
In tangled roots, our pasts connect,
With every chuckle that we collect.

The Silent Network

Beneath the soil, a buzz goes round,
A secret chat that can't be found.
Mushrooms texting, 'Have you heard?',
While snails are crafting tales absurd.

A leafy grape vine starts the tease,
'Did you see that guy? He slipped with ease!'
The daisies laugh, their petals shaking,
As earthworms join in, their laughter waking.

'Watch your step!' a toadstool shouts,
As squirrels roll by, fueling doubts.
The laughter ripples through the glade,
Underground humor, never afraid.

So tiptoe soft 'round here, my friend,
You never know what jokes will blend.
Life's a comedy, just press record,
In the silent network, laughter's stored.

Life's Uncharted Depths

In caverns dark where treasures hide,
A gopher maps out a goofy ride.
He draws the lines with dainty paws,
While pondering life's silly laws.

What's under me? A pancake feast?
With syrup rivers, I am released!
The worms say, 'Join us, don't be shy!'
As cacti chuckle and stand by.

The bubbles burst with bubbly cheer,
As roots high-five, 'We're pioneers!'
Invisible bits throw a grand ball,
Inviting everyone, big and small.

So journey deep where laughter flows,
In the depths of earth, fun only grows.
With every giggle and little dance,
Life's a silly, underground romance.

www.ingramcontent.com/pod-product-compliance
Lightning Source LLC
Chambersburg PA
CBHW050307120526
44590CB00016B/2521